Workbook for
New Marriage, Same Couple

Disclaimer:

This workbook provides insights and suggestions for navigating challenging phases in a marriage. The content is based on general principles and experiences and does not guarantee specific outcomes. Readers are encouraged to exercise discretion and seek professional advice when needed. The author and publisher are not responsible for individual actions or the results of applying the concepts presented.

How to Use This Workbook

Welcome to our workbook! This workbook is designed to help you implement the teachings from the accompanying book into practical exercises. Follow this guide to maximize your learning experience.

Workbook Structure

Short Answer Questions:

Throughout the workbook, you'll find short answer questions related to each chapter. Use these questions to reflect on the key concepts and apply them to your personal or professional life.

Chapter Summaries:

After each set of questions, you'll find a chapter summary. This provides a brief overview of the main concepts discussed in the corresponding chapter of the book.

Key Takeaways:

Extracted from the book, the key takeaways highlight the crucial points you should focus on. Keep these in mind as you progress through the workbook.

How to Get Started

Read the Book First:

It is highly recommended to read the corresponding chapter in the book before attempting the workbook exercises. This will provide you with the necessary context for a deeper understanding.

Answer Questions Thoughtfully:

Take your time to answer the short answer questions. The more thoughtful and detailed your responses, the more you'll benefit from the exercises.

Review Chapter Summaries:

Before moving on to the next set of questions, review the chapter summary. This will reinforce the main ideas and help you connect them to your responses.

Apply Key Takeaways:

Use the key takeaways as a guide for practical application. Consider how you can integrate these lessons into your daily life or work.

Tips for Success

Consistency is Key:

Work through the workbook consistently to build a strong understanding of the book's teachings.

Reflect on Your Progress:

Periodically reflect on your responses and progress. Celebrate your achievements and identify areas for improvement.

Reach Out for Clarifications:

If you encounter challenges or have questions, don't hesitate to refer back to the book or seek additional resources. Learning is a journey, and clarification can enhance your experience.

Chapter 1: Cracks in the Camelot: Recognizing the Shift

Overview:

In this foundational chapter, the author explores the early stages of marriage, emphasizing the common challenges couples face as they navigate the transition from the honeymoon phase to the reality of everyday life. The focus is on recognizing the signs of strain, identifying turning points, and understanding the impact on the relationship.

Key Takeaways:
Early Honeymoon Phase and Unrealistic Expectations
Teaching Points:
Idealized Beginning:

The chapter begins by acknowledging the idealized nature of the early honeymoon phase. Couples often enter marriage with high expectations, fueled by the excitement and romance of the initial stages.
Unrealistic Expectations:

Readers are guided to explore the unrealistic expectations that can accompany the honeymoon phase. These expectations may revolve around constant bliss, perfect communication, and unending romance, setting the stage for potential disappointment.
Main Lesson:
The author aims to teach that the early stages of marriage are often characterized by an idealized perception. Recognizing the presence of unrealistic expectations is crucial for couples to navigate the shift in dynamics and set realistic foundations for their relationship.

a. Reflect on the early days of your relationship. Write about the positive aspects and feelings during the honeymoon phase. Consider any unrealistic expectations that may have been present.

_____

_____

_____

_____

_____

_____

_____

_____

_____

_____

_____

_____

_____

_____

b. Identify specific expectations you had for your partner or the relationship early on. Write about how these expectations may have contributed to the honeymoon phase and how they evolved over time. Consider realistic adjustments you can make.

_____

_____

_____

_____

_____

_____

_____

_____

_____

_____

_____

_____

_____

c. Consider your current expectations in the relationship. Write about how they have changed since the early days. Develop a list of realistic expectations that align with the reality of a long-term relationship.

_____

_____

_____

_____

_____

_____

_____

_____

_____

_____

_____

_____

_____

_____

_____

Identifying the Turning Point and Its Impact on the Relationship
Teaching Points:
Transition Period:

The chapter explores the turning point that marks the transition from the honeymoon phase to a more mature stage of the relationship. This turning point is often accompanied by various challenges and adjustments.
Impact on Dynamics:

Readers are guided to understand the impact of the turning point on the dynamics of the relationship. This may include shifts in communication, intimacy, and overall interaction between partners.
Main Lesson:
The turning point is a pivotal moment in the marriage, signaling a shift from the initial romantic phase to a more realistic and complex stage. Understanding and navigating this transition is essential for couples to grow and adapt in their relationship.

a. Write about a specific turning point or significant event in your relationship. Reflect on how this event marked a shift from the honeymoon phase to a more nuanced reality. Consider the impact on both partners.

_____

_____

_____

_____

_____

_____

_____

_____

_____

_____

_____

_____

_____

_____

_____

b. Identify any challenges or conflicts that arose during the turning point. Write about how these challenges were navigated and the lessons learned. Consider how addressing these challenges can contribute to the health of the relationship.

_____

_____

_____

_____

_____

_____

_____

_____

_____

_____

_____

_____

_____

_____

c. Consider the emotional and communication dynamics during the turning point. Write about the impact on intimacy and connection. Develop strategies for maintaining emotional closeness during challenging times.

_____

_____

_____

_____

_____

_____

_____

_____

_____

_____

_____

_____

_____

_____

Common Warning Signs of Marital Struggles
Teaching Points:
Communication Breakdown:

The chapter highlights common warning signs, such as communication breakdowns, that indicate underlying marital struggles. Issues like miscommunication, unexpressed expectations, and unresolved conflicts are explored.
Emotional Distance:

Emotional distance is discussed as a potential warning sign. The author delves into how couples may drift apart emotionally, leading to a sense of disconnection.
Main Lesson:
By identifying common warning signs, couples can proactively address potential challenges. The chapter teaches the importance of recognizing these signs early on to prevent deeper marital struggles and foster a healthier relationship.

a. Reflect on any recent conflicts or tensions in your relationship. Write about common warning signs that may have preceded these struggles. Consider how early recognition of these signs can lead to proactive resolution.

_____

_____

_____

_____

_____

_____

_____

_____

_____

_____

_____

_____

_____

_____

b. Identify patterns of communication breakdowns in your relationship. Write about how these patterns may indicate potential struggles. Develop a plan for improving communication to prevent escalating conflicts.

_____

_____

_____

_____

_____

_____

_____

_____

_____

_____

_____

_____

_____

c. Consider the emotional well-being of both partners. Write about signs of emotional distance or distress. Develop strategies for fostering emotional connection and support during times of marital struggles.

_____

_____

_____

_____

_____

_____

_____

_____

_____

_____

_____

_____

_____

Chapter 2: The Blame Game: Whose Fault Is It Anyway?

Overview:

In this insightful chapter, the author tackles the destructive dynamics of blame within a marriage. The focus is on understanding the futility of blame, shifting from a "why" mentality to a constructive "how" approach, and embracing individual responsibility and personal growth as catalysts for positive change.

Key Takeaways:

Understanding the Futility of Blame and Finger-Pointing

Teaching Points:

Blame as a Destructive Force:

The chapter begins by highlighting the detrimental impact of blame on a marriage. Finger-pointing and assigning fault create a toxic atmosphere, hindering communication and connection between partners.

Cycle of Recrimination:

Readers are guided to recognize the cyclical nature of blame, where accusations lead to defensiveness, escalating conflicts without addressing underlying issues.

Main Lesson:

The author aims to convey that blame is a counterproductive force in a marriage. Understanding its futility is crucial for couples to break free from destructive patterns and create a healthier relational environment.

a. Reflect on a recent situation where blame and finger-pointing occurred in your relationship. Write about the emotions and consequences that resulted from this blame game. Consider the futility of assigning blame in resolving conflicts.

_____

_____

_____

_____

_____

_____

_____

_____

_____

_____

_____

_____

_____

_____

_____

b. Identify recurring patterns of blame within your relationship. Write about the impact on trust and communication. Consider alternative approaches to conflict resolution that move away from blaming and focus on constructive solutions.

_____

_____

_____

_____

_____

_____

_____

_____

_____

_____

_____

_____

_____

_____

_____

c. Consider a specific challenge you and your partner are currently facing. Write about the potential consequences of engaging in the blame game. Develop a plan for reframing the conversation towards collaborative problem-solving.

_____

_____

_____

_____

_____

_____

_____

_____

_____

_____

_____

_____

_____

Shifting Focus from "Why" to "How" to Move Forward

Teaching Points:

Transitioning Questions:

The chapter encourages a shift in mindset from dwelling on "why" blame occurs to asking "how" the couple can move forward constructively. Shifting the focus to solutions opens the door to positive change.

Collaborative Problem-Solving:

Practical strategies are provided for collaborative problem-solving. The lesson emphasizes the importance of working together to find solutions rather than placing blame.

Main Lesson:

By transitioning from "why" to "how," couples can redirect their energy toward finding solutions and building a stronger foundation. This shift in focus fosters a collaborative approach to problem-solving and mutual growth.

a. Think about a recent disagreement where the focus was on "why" the issue occurred. Write about the challenges and obstacles this approach presented. Consider how shifting the focus to "how" to move forward can be more productive.

_____

_____

_____

_____

_____

_____

_____

_____

_____

_____

_____

_____

_____

_____

_____

b. Identify a recurring issue in your relationship. Write about the reasons behind this issue and the impact of continually asking "why." Develop a list of actionable steps you can take to shift the focus towards finding constructive solutions.

_____

_____

_____

_____

_____

_____

_____

_____

_____

_____

_____

_____

_____

_____

c. Reflect on a successful resolution to a past conflict. Write about how the shift from "why" to "how" played a role in reaching a positive outcome. Develop a habit of incorporating this approach into future conflict resolutions.

_____

_____

_____

_____

_____

_____

_____

_____

_____

_____

_____

_____

_____

_____

Individual Responsibility and Personal Growth
Teaching Points:
Owning Personal Actions:

The chapter explores the concept of individual responsibility. Each partner is encouraged to own their actions, fostering a sense of accountability for personal contributions to the relationship.
Embracing Personal Growth:

Readers are guided on the importance of personal growth within the marriage. The lesson emphasizes that individual development contributes to the overall health and vitality of the relationship.
Main Lesson:
The author teaches that embracing individual responsibility and committing to personal growth are essential components of a thriving marriage. Couples are empowered to take ownership of their actions and actively pursue personal development.

a. Reflect on a situation where taking individual responsibility led to personal growth. Write about the positive outcomes and the impact on your relationship. Consider areas where you can take more responsibility for personal growth.

_____

_____

_____

_____

_____

_____

_____

_____

_____

_____

_____

_____

_____

_____

b. Identify a challenge in your relationship where both partners can take individual responsibility. Write about the specific actions each person can take to contribute to personal growth and relationship improvement.

_____

_____

_____

_____

_____

_____

_____

_____

_____

_____

_____

_____

_____

_____

c. Consider your own personal growth goals. Write about how achieving these goals can positively impact your relationship. Develop a plan for integrating personal development into your relationship journey, fostering growth for both partners.

_____

_____

_____

_____

_____

_____

_____

_____

_____

_____

_____

_____

_____

_____

Chapter 3: The Brink of Despair: Is There Hope?

Overview:

In this poignant chapter, the author addresses the critical juncture when couples find themselves on the brink of despair in their marriage. The focus is on confronting feelings of hopelessness, rediscovering the reasons for committing to the marriage, and unlocking the transformative power of hope to move forward.

Key Takeaways:
Confronting Feelings of Hopelessness and Despair
Teaching Points:
Acknowledging Emotions:

The chapter begins by acknowledging the intense emotions of hopelessness and despair that couples may experience. Readers are encouraged to confront these emotions openly and honestly.
Impact on the Marriage:

The author explores how feelings of despair can negatively impact the marriage, leading to a sense of disconnection and the questioning of the relationship's viability.
Main Lesson:
By acknowledging and confronting feelings of hopelessness, couples can initiate a process of honest self-reflection and communication. This is the first step toward understanding the root causes of despair and seeking solutions.

a. Write about a specific moment or situation where you felt hopeless in your relationship. Explore the emotions and thoughts associated with this despair. Consider the impact on your mental and emotional well-being.

_____

_____

_____

_____

_____

_____

_____

_____

_____

_____

_____

_____

_____

_____

b. Reflect on recurring patterns of despair in your relationship. Write about the triggers and common themes. Develop strategies for confronting these feelings when they arise, focusing on self-awareness and emotional regulation.

_____

_____

_____

_____

_____

_____

_____

_____

_____

_____

_____

_____

_____

_____

_____

c. Consider the impact of hopelessness on your communication with your partner. Write about how despair may lead to withdrawal or conflict. Develop a plan for maintaining open communication even during challenging times.

_____

_____

_____

_____

_____

_____

_____

_____

_____

_____

_____

_____

_____

_____

Rediscovering the Reasons for Committing to the Marriage

Teaching Points:
Reflecting on Commitment:

The chapter guides couples in reflecting on the initial reasons for committing to the marriage. This involves revisiting the shared values, aspirations, and love that brought them together.

Assessing the Journey:

Practical exercises are introduced to help couples assess the journey they have traveled together. This includes recognizing challenges, celebrating successes, and understanding the evolution of the relationship.

Main Lesson:

Rediscovering the reasons for commitment serves as a powerful anchor during moments of despair. The chapter teaches that reflecting on the foundation of the marriage can rekindle a sense of purpose and connection.

a. Reflect on the initial reasons you committed to your marriage. Write about the qualities and aspects that initially attracted you to your partner. Reconnect with the positive emotions associated with those early commitments.

_____

_____

_____

_____

_____

_____

_____

_____

_____

_____

_____

_____

_____

_____

_____

b. Identify specific challenges in your relationship that have led to feelings of doubt. Write about the reasons you initially chose to overcome these challenges. Revisit your commitment and find strength in the initial motivations for your marriage.

_____

_____

_____

_____

_____

_____

_____

_____

_____

_____

_____

_____

_____

_____

c. Consider your current priorities and values within the marriage. Write about how these align with the reasons for committing to the relationship. Develop a renewed sense of purpose by rediscovering and reaffirming your commitment.

_____

_____

_____

_____

_____

_____

_____

_____

_____

_____

_____

_____

_____

_____

_____

Finding the Spark of Hope and Its Power to Move Forward
Teaching Points:
Recognizing Sparks of Hope:

The lesson explores how even in the darkest moments, there are sparks of hope. Readers are encouraged to identify and nurture these sparks as potential sources of positive transformation.
Hope as a Catalyst:

The transformative power of hope is emphasized. The author discusses how cultivating hope can become a catalyst for change, inspiring couples to actively work towards a renewed and strengthened marriage.
Main Lesson:
Finding and cultivating the spark of hope is essential for moving forward. The chapter teaches that hope is not only a beacon in difficult times but also a dynamic force that empowers couples to navigate challenges with resilience and determination.

a. Write about a moment when you felt a spark of hope in your relationship. Explore the factors that contributed to this hopeful feeling. Consider how harnessing this spark can influence positive change.

_____

_____

_____

_____

_____

_____

_____

_____

_____

_____

_____

_____

_____

_____

b. Reflect on past instances where hope played a role in overcoming challenges. Write about the specific actions you and your partner took to move forward. Develop a plan for fostering hope as a catalyst for growth.

_____

_____

_____

_____

_____

_____

_____

_____

_____

_____

_____

_____

_____

_____

c. Consider a current challenge in your marriage. Write about potential solutions and positive outcomes. Focus on finding the spark of hope even in difficult times, recognizing its power to inspire resilience and progress.

_____

_____

_____

_____

_____

_____

_____

_____

_____

_____

_____

_____

_____

_____

Chapter 4: Start with You: Taking Ownership of Your Journey

Overview:

In this transformative chapter, the author guides couples on a journey of self-discovery and personal responsibility within the context of their marriage. The focus is on understanding that personal change has a profound impact on the entire relationship, identifying individual issues and growth areas, and committing to self-work and personal transformation as a means to enhance the marriage.

Key Takeaways:
Understanding That Personal Change Affects the Entire Relationship
Teaching Points:
Interconnectedness of Individual and Relationship Growth:

The chapter emphasizes the interconnected nature of individual growth and the health of the marriage. Readers are guided to recognize that personal change has a ripple effect, influencing the dynamics and well-being of the entire relationship.
Shifting the Focus Inward:

Practical insights are provided to shift the focus from blaming external factors to looking inward. By understanding the role of personal attitudes and behaviors, couples can pave the way for positive change in the relationship.
Main Lesson:
The author aims to convey that personal change is a catalyst for relationship growth. By recognizing the impact of individual attitudes and actions, couples can embark on a shared journey of transformation.

a. Reflect on a time when personal changes positively impacted your relationship. Write about the specific behaviors or attitudes you worked on and the subsequent impact on your partner and the relationship.

_____

_____

_____

_____

_____

_____

_____

_____

_____

_____

_____

_____

_____

_____

b. Identify a current challenge in your relationship. Write about how personal changes, either positive or negative, may be influencing the dynamic. Consider the ripple effect of individual actions on the overall relationship.

_____

_____

_____

_____

_____

_____

_____

_____

_____

_____

_____

_____

_____

_____

c. Consider the role of communication in personal change. Write about how discussing personal growth with your partner can enhance understanding and support. Develop a plan for open and honest communication about individual journeys within the relationship.

_____

_____

_____

_____

_____

_____

_____

_____

_____

_____

_____

_____

_____

Identifying Individual Issues and Areas for Growth
Teaching Points:
Self-Reflection:

The chapter encourages couples to engage in honest self-reflection. Readers are guided to identify individual issues, patterns, and behaviors that may contribute to challenges within the marriage.

Growth Opportunities:

Practical exercises are introduced to help couples pinpoint areas for personal growth. This involves assessing strengths and weaknesses, acknowledging areas of improvement, and setting goals for individual development.

Main Lesson:

Identifying individual issues and growth areas is an essential step in the process of self-discovery. The chapter teaches that by addressing these aspects, couples can create a foundation for positive change in both themselves and the relationship.

a. Write about a specific issue or pattern in your behavior that may be affecting the relationship. Reflect on how this issue aligns with your personal values and growth goals. Develop strategies for addressing and overcoming this challenge.

_____

_____

_____

_____

_____

_____

_____

_____

_____

_____

_____

_____

_____

_____

_____

b. Identify recurring themes or conflicts in your relationship. Write about the underlying issues or triggers that contribute to these conflicts. Develop a plan for personal growth to address these root causes and break negative patterns.

_____

_____

_____

_____

_____

_____

_____

_____

_____

_____

_____

_____

_____

_____

_____

c. Consider your strengths and weaknesses as an individual. Write about areas where you can further develop and grow. Develop actionable steps for self-improvement that align with your values and contribute to a healthier relationship.

_____

_____

_____

_____

_____

_____

_____

_____

_____

_____

_____

_____

_____

_____

Committing to Self-Work and Personal Transformation
Teaching Points:
Active Engagement in Self-Work:

The lesson guides couples in committing to self-work as an ongoing process. This includes adopting a growth mindset, seeking self-improvement resources, and actively engaging in practices that foster personal transformation.

Individual Responsibility for Change:

Readers are encouraged to take ownership of their journey and recognize that personal transformation is a responsibility that each partner bears. The chapter promotes the idea that individuals have the power to shape their own growth.

Main Lesson:

Committing to self-work and personal transformation is the key to a thriving marriage. The chapter teaches that by actively engaging in the process of self-improvement, couples not only enhance their individual lives but also contribute positively to the relationship.

a. Write about your motivation for committing to self-work and personal transformation. Reflect on the positive impact this commitment can have on your relationship. Develop a vision of the person you aim to become.

_____

_____

_____

_____

_____

_____

_____

_____

_____

_____

_____

_____

_____

_____

b. Consider past attempts at personal transformation. Write about the strategies that were effective and those that were not. Develop a plan for approaching self-work with resilience and adaptability.

_____

_____

_____

_____

_____

_____

_____

_____

_____

_____

_____

_____

_____

_____

_____

c. Reflect on the support systems available to you in your personal transformation journey. Write about how your partner, friends, or mentors can contribute to your growth. Develop a plan for actively seeking and utilizing support in your journey.

_____

_____

_____

_____

_____

_____

_____

_____

_____

_____

_____

_____

_____

_____

Chapter 5: Take Quitting off the Table: Choosing Commitment

Overview:

In this pivotal chapter, the author addresses the common temptation to give up on a marriage when faced with challenges. The focus is on recognizing this temptation, recommitting to the vows made, and providing practical strategies for staying present and invested in the marriage despite difficulties.

Key Takeaways:

Recognizing the Temptation to Give Up When Things Get Tough

Teaching Points:

Understanding Normal Challenges:

The chapter begins by normalizing the challenges that every marriage faces. Readers are guided to recognize that difficulties are a natural part of any relationship, and the temptation to quit can arise during tough times.

Impact of External Pressures:

The author explores how external pressures, such as societal expectations or the influence of others, can contribute to the temptation to give up. Readers are encouraged to differentiate between external influences and the intrinsic value of their commitment.

Main Lesson:

The author aims to convey that recognizing the temptation to quit is the first step toward building resilience in a marriage. By understanding the commonality of this challenge, couples can approach difficulties with a renewed commitment to navigate them together.

a. Reflect on a challenging period in your relationship where giving up seemed like an option. Write about the emotions and thoughts associated with that temptation. Identify specific triggers or stressors that contributed to these feelings.

_____

_____

_____

_____

_____

_____

_____

_____

_____

_____

_____

_____

_____

_____

b. Identify recurring patterns or situations that trigger thoughts of giving up. Write about the impact of these patterns on your commitment. Develop a plan for recognizing and addressing these triggers when they arise.

_____

_____

_____

_____

_____

_____

_____

_____

_____

_____

_____

_____

_____

_____

c. Consider the role of external influences on your relationship. Write about how societal expectations or the experiences of others may contribute to the temptation to give up. Develop a mindset that separates external pressures from your commitment to the marriage.

Recommitting to the Vows and Fighting for the Future
You Envision
Teaching Points:
Revisiting Vows and Commitments:

The chapter guides couples in revisiting the vows made during their commitment. This involves reflecting on the promises to love, honor, and support each other through thick and thin.
Fighting for a Shared Future:

Practical insights are provided on fighting for the future envisioned together. Couples are encouraged to align their actions with the shared goals and dreams that initially brought them together.
Main Lesson:
Recommitting to vows and fighting for a shared future is an active choice. The chapter teaches that by embracing this commitment, couples can overcome challenges and work towards a marriage that reflects their shared vision.

a. Write about the specific aspects of your vows that resonate with you. Reflect on the initial commitment you made to your partner. Develop a renewed sense of connection to the essence of your vows.

_____

_____

_____

_____

_____

_____

_____

_____

_____

_____

_____

_____

_____

_____

b. Identify the future you envision for your relationship. Write about the goals and aspirations you share
with your partner. Develop a plan for actively working
towards this future, reinforcing your commitment to
building a life together.

_____

_____

_____

_____

_____

_____

_____

_____

_____

_____

_____

_____

_____

_____

c. Consider a challenging aspect of your relationship. Write about the specific actions you can take to address this challenge and contribute to a positive future. Develop strategies for fighting for the future you envision, even during difficult times.

_____

_____

_____

_____

_____

_____

_____

_____

_____

_____

_____

_____

_____

_____

Practical Strategies for Staying Present and Invested in the Marriage
Teaching Points:
Staying Present in Difficult Moments:

The lesson explores practical strategies for staying present during challenging times. This involves mindfulness techniques, effective communication, and a focus on the present rather than dwelling on past grievances.
Investing Time and Effort:

Practical actions for investing time and effort into the marriage are discussed. The chapter emphasizes the importance of intentional acts of love, quality time together, and ongoing communication.
Main Lesson:
Staying present and invested in the marriage requires conscious effort. The chapter teaches that practical strategies, when consistently applied, contribute to the resilience of the relationship and strengthen the bond between partners.

a. Write about the distractions or external pressures that often take your focus away from the present moment in your relationship. Develop strategies for staying present, such as setting boundaries, practicing mindfulness, or scheduling quality time.

_____

_____

_____

_____

_____

_____

_____

_____

_____

_____

_____

_____

_____

_____

b. Reflect on past moments of disconnection or detachment. Write about the impact on your relationship and personal well-being. Develop practical strategies for staying invested in the marriage, fostering a sense of connection and closeness.

_____

_____

_____

_____

_____

_____

_____

_____

_____

_____

_____

_____

_____

_____

c. Consider the role of shared experiences in staying present. Write about activities or rituals that strengthen your bond as a couple. Develop a plan for incorporating these shared experiences into your routine, creating opportunities for connection and investment.

_____

_____

_____

_____

_____

_____

_____

_____

_____

_____

_____

_____

_____

_____

_____

Chapter 6: Allow Others In: Building a Support System

Overview:

In this chapter, the author emphasizes the importance of breaking the taboo of seeking help and vulnerability within a marriage. The focus is on choosing trustworthy confidantes and mentors, as well as recognizing the valuable role of professional therapy and community support in strengthening the marital bond.

Key Takeaways:
Breaking the Taboo of Seeking Help and Vulnerability
Teaching Points:
Challenging Societal Norms:

The chapter begins by challenging societal norms that may stigmatize seeking help in a marriage. Readers are encouraged to break free from the taboo associated with vulnerability and recognize the strength in reaching out for support.

Normalizing Help-Seeking:

Practical insights are provided to normalize the act of seeking help. The author emphasizes that asking for assistance is a courageous step and does not diminish the strength of the marriage but rather enhances it.

Main Lesson:

The author aims to convey that breaking the taboo of seeking help is a powerful act of resilience. By embracing vulnerability and seeking support, couples can navigate challenges with greater understanding and resources.

a. Write about any cultural or personal taboos around seeking help or showing vulnerability that you may have internalized. Reflect on the impact of these taboos on your willingness to reach out for support during challenging times.

_____

_____

_____

_____

_____

_____

_____

_____

_____

_____

_____

_____

_____

_____

_____

b. Identify specific situations in your relationship where seeking help or being vulnerable was challenging. Write about the emotions and thoughts associated with these moments. Develop a plan for breaking through these barriers and embracing vulnerability.

_____

_____

_____

_____

_____

_____

_____

_____

_____

_____

_____

_____

_____

_____

c. Consider the potential benefits of seeking help and being vulnerable in your relationship. Write about how opening up can strengthen connections and foster understanding. Develop a mindset that values the courage and strength in seeking support.

_____

_____

_____

_____

_____

_____

_____

_____

_____

_____

_____

_____

_____

_____

Choosing Trustworthy Confidantes and Mentors
Teaching Points:
Selecting Supportive Individuals:

The chapter guides couples in choosing trustworthy confidantes and mentors. This involves identifying individuals who are supportive, non-judgmental, and capable of providing valuable insights.

Communication with Spouse:

Practical advice is provided on communicating with one's spouse about the intention to seek support. The lesson emphasizes the importance of transparency and mutual agreement when involving others in the marital journey.

Main Lesson:

Choosing confidantes and mentors wisely is crucial for effective support. The chapter teaches that by fostering open communication and selecting supportive individuals, couples can strengthen their connection and benefit from external perspectives.

a. Reflect on past experiences where you sought advice or shared your challenges with others. Write about the impact of choosing trustworthy confidantes. Consider the qualities that make someone trustworthy in this role.

_____

_____

_____

_____

_____

_____

_____

_____

_____

_____

_____

_____

_____

_____

b. Identify potential confidantes or mentors in your life. Write about the qualities and characteristics that make them trustworthy. Develop a plan for building or strengthening these relationships to create a reliable support system.

_____

_____

_____

_____

_____

_____

_____

_____

_____

_____

_____

_____

_____

_____

_____

c. Consider the role of reciprocity in confidante and mentor relationships. Write about how you can contribute to the well-being of others in your support system. Develop a mindset of mutual support and shared growth.

_____

_____

_____

_____

_____

_____

_____

_____

_____

_____

_____

_____

_____

_____

_____

The Role of Professional Therapy and Community Support
Teaching Points:
Professional Therapy as a Resource:

The lesson explores the role of professional therapy as a valuable resource. Readers are guided to consider therapy as a proactive and constructive step towards resolving challenges and improving communication.
Community Support Networks:

The chapter highlights the significance of community support networks. Engaging with like-minded individuals or participating in community activities can provide couples with a sense of belonging and shared experiences.
Main Lesson:
Recognizing the role of professional therapy and community support is essential for comprehensive marital health. The chapter teaches that accessing these resources can bring new perspectives, tools, and a sense of community to the marriage.

a. Write about any hesitations or reservations you may have about seeking professional therapy. Reflect on the potential benefits and the role it can play in supporting your relationship. Develop a plan for overcoming hesitations and considering therapy as a valuable resource.

_____

_____

_____

_____

_____

_____

_____

_____

_____

_____

_____

_____

_____

b. Identify community support networks that align with your values and interests. Write about the potential benefits of engaging with these communities. Develop a plan for actively participating and contributing to community support.

_____

_____

_____

_____

_____

_____

_____

_____

_____

_____

_____

_____

_____

_____

c. Consider the role of professional therapy as a preventive measure rather than a last resort. Write about how regular check-ins with a therapist can contribute to the health of your relationship. Develop a proactive mindset towards therapy as a tool for ongoing growth and resilience.

_____

_____

_____

_____

_____

_____

_____

_____

_____

_____

_____

_____

_____

Chapter 7: Yield to Vision: Reimagining Your Future Together

Overview:

In this transformative chapter, the author guides couples in setting clear goals and crafting a shared vision for the future of their marriage. The focus is on rekindling individual and shared dreams, aspirations, and cultivating hope. The chapter encourages couples to believe in the possibilities of renewal and actively participate in the creation of a future that aligns with their shared vision.

Key Takeaways:

Setting Clear Goals and a Shared Vision for the Future of the Marriage

Teaching Points:

Goal-Setting as a Collaborative Process:

The chapter emphasizes the importance of collaborative goal-setting. Couples are guided to engage in open and honest communication to establish clear goals for their individual and shared future.

Shared Vision as a Foundation:

Practical insights are provided on creating a shared vision. The lesson underscores the idea that a shared vision acts as a foundation for the marriage, providing direction and purpose.

Main Lesson:

The author aims to convey that setting clear goals and a shared vision is an active and intentional process. By aligning their aspirations and working together towards common objectives, couples can reinvigorate their sense of purpose and direction.

a. Reflect on your current goals as a couple. Write about the clarity and specificity of these goals. Consider how well-defined goals contribute to a sense of direction and purpose in your relationship.

_____

_____

_____

_____

_____

_____

_____

_____

_____

_____

_____

_____

_____

_____

_____

b. Identify areas in your marriage where a shared vision is lacking. Write about the impact of not having a unified direction. Develop specific goals that align with your individual values and contribute to a shared vision for the future.

_____

_____

_____

_____

_____

_____

_____

_____

_____

_____

_____

_____

_____

_____

c. Consider a challenging aspect of your relationship. Write about how setting clear goals can address or overcome this challenge. Develop an action plan for collaboratively setting and working towards these goals.

_____

_____

_____

_____

_____

_____

_____

_____

_____

_____

_____

_____

_____

_____

_____

Rekindling Individual and Shared Dreams and Aspirations
Teaching Points:
Individual Dreams and Aspirations:

The chapter encourages couples to rekindle individual dreams and aspirations. Readers are guided to reflect on personal goals and desires, recognizing that individual fulfillment contributes to the overall health of the marriage.
Rediscovering Shared Dreams:

Practical exercises are introduced to help couples rediscover shared dreams. This involves revisiting past aspirations, exploring new possibilities, and aligning their collective vision for the future.
Main Lesson:
Rekindling both individual and shared dreams is essential for the vitality of the marriage. The chapter teaches that by nurturing personal aspirations and fostering a joint sense of purpose, couples can create a dynamic and fulfilling future together.

a. Write about your individual dreams and aspirations that may have taken a backseat in the relationship. Reflect on the importance of pursuing personal goals alongside shared aspirations. Develop a plan for rekindling and pursuing these individual dreams.

_____

_____

_____

_____

_____

_____

_____

_____

_____

_____

_____

_____

_____

_____

b. Identify shared dreams or aspirations that have faded over time. Write about the factors that contributed to this fading. Develop strategies for reigniting and actively working towards these shared goals.

_____

_____

_____

_____

_____

_____

_____

_____

_____

_____

_____

_____

_____

_____

c. Consider the role of communication in understanding each other's dreams. Write about how open dialogue and active listening can enhance the understanding of individual and shared aspirations. Develop communication habits that foster a supportive environment for expressing dreams.

_____

_____

_____

_____

_____

_____

_____

_____

_____

_____

_____

_____

_____

_____

Cultivating Hope and Believing in the Possibilities of Renewal

Teaching Points:

Hope as a Driving Force:

The lesson explores the transformative power of hope. Couples are guided to cultivate hope as a driving force that fuels their belief in the possibilities of renewal and positive change.

Mindset Shift towards Possibilities:

Practical strategies are provided for cultivating a mindset shift towards possibilities. This involves reframing challenges as opportunities for growth and renewal, fostering a positive outlook on the future.

Main Lesson:

Cultivating hope is a foundational element for reimagining the future of the marriage. The chapter teaches that by embracing hope, couples can overcome challenges with resilience and approach their shared journey with optimism.

a. Reflect on a challenging period in your relationship. Write about the role of hope in navigating that difficulty. Consider how cultivating hope can contribute to resilience and the belief in the possibilities of renewal.

_____

_____

_____

_____

_____

_____

_____

_____

_____

_____

_____

_____

_____

_____

b. Identify specific actions or behaviors that have eroded hope in your relationship. Write about the impact of hopelessness on your connection. Develop a plan for replacing negative patterns with hope-affirming behaviors.

_____

_____

_____

_____

_____

_____

_____

_____

_____

_____

_____

_____

_____

_____

c. Consider a shared vision for the future. Write about how this vision inspires hope and belief in the possibilities of renewal. Develop rituals or practices that regularly reinforce this vision, cultivating a sense of optimism and shared purpose.

_____

_____

_____

_____

_____

_____

_____

_____

_____

_____

_____

_____

_____

_____

Chapter 8: The Journey Is the Reward: Learning to Love Again

Overview:

In this concluding chapter, the author guides couples through the process of rebuilding a marriage, emphasizing that the journey itself is a rewarding experience. The focus is on recognizing that rebuilding takes time and consistent effort, celebrating small victories, and practicing gratitude to rediscover joy in the simple things. The chapter encourages couples to embrace the transformative power of love as they navigate the ongoing journey of renewal.

Key Takeaways:
Recognizing That Rebuilding Takes Time and Consistent Effort
Teaching Points:
Patience as a Virtue:

The chapter begins by highlighting the virtue of patience in the process of rebuilding a marriage. Readers are guided to recognize that healing and transformation take time and require consistent effort.

Understanding the Gradual Nature of Change:

Practical insights are provided on understanding the gradual nature of change. The lesson emphasizes that small, consistent steps contribute to the overall evolution of the relationship.

Main Lesson:

The author aims to convey that rebuilding a marriage is not an instantaneous process. The chapter teaches that patience, coupled with consistent effort, is key to achieving lasting positive change.

a. Reflect on your expectations regarding the timeline for rebuilding your marriage. Write about any impatience or pressure you may be placing on the process. Develop a realistic timeline and commitment to consistent effort.

_____

_____

_____

_____

_____

_____

_____

_____

_____

_____

_____

_____

_____

_____

b. Identify specific areas in your relationship that require rebuilding. Write about the challenges and setbacks you've encountered. Develop a plan for breaking down these areas into manageable steps and consistently working towards improvement.

_____

_____

_____

_____

_____

_____

_____

_____

_____

_____

_____

_____

_____

_____

c. Consider the role of communication in the rebuilding process. Write about how ongoing dialogue and feedback contribute to understanding and growth. Develop communication habits that support the consistent effort required for rebuilding.

_____

_____

_____

_____

_____

_____

_____

_____

_____

_____

_____

_____

_____

_____

Celebrating Small Victories and Milestones Along the Way

Teaching Points:

Acknowledging Progress:

The chapter encourages couples to acknowledge and celebrate small victories. Recognizing progress, no matter how incremental, contributes to a positive and motivating atmosphere within the marriage.

Milestones as Markers of Growth:

Practical exercises are introduced to help couples identify and appreciate milestones in their journey. Celebrating these markers becomes a way of acknowledging the growth and evolution of the relationship.

Main Lesson:

Celebrating small victories and milestones is a vital aspect of the rebuilding process. The chapter teaches that these celebrations create a sense of achievement and reinforce the couple's commitment to positive change.

a. Write about a recent small victory or positive change in your relationship. Reflect on the impact of celebrating these moments. Develop a habit of recognizing and acknowledging small victories regularly.

_____

_____

_____

_____

_____

_____

_____

_____

_____

_____

_____

_____

_____

_____

b. Identify milestones you hope to achieve in the re-building process. Write about the significance of each milestone. Develop a plan for celebrating these milestones as a couple, fostering a sense of accomplishment and progress.

_____

_____

_____

_____

_____

_____

_____

_____

_____

_____

_____

_____

_____

_____

c. Consider the role of mutual celebration in strengthening your connection. Write about how acknowledging each other's efforts contributes to a supportive environment. Develop a routine for expressing gratitude and celebrating achievements together.

_____

_____

_____

_____

_____

_____

_____

_____

_____

_____

_____

_____

_____

_____

Practicing Gratitude and Rediscovering Joy in the Simple Things

Teaching Points:

Gratitude as a Transformative Practice:

The lesson explores the transformative power of gratitude. Couples are guided to practice gratitude as a means of appreciating and valuing each other, fostering a positive and supportive atmosphere.

Rediscovering Joy in Everyday Moments:

Practical strategies are provided for rediscovering joy in simple, everyday moments. The chapter emphasizes the importance of finding happiness in the journey rather than solely focusing on destination goals.

Main Lesson:

Practicing gratitude and rediscovering joy in the simple things is fundamental to a renewed marriage. The chapter teaches that by cultivating a mindset of appreciation, couples can enhance their connection and find fulfillment in the present moment.

a. Write about specific aspects of your relationship or partner that you are grateful for. Reflect on the positive impact of practicing gratitude. Develop a routine for expressing appreciation regularly.

_____

_____

_____

_____

_____

_____

_____

_____

_____

_____

_____

_____

_____

b. Identify simple activities or moments that bring joy to your relationship. Write about the importance of rediscovering joy in everyday life. Develop a plan for incorporating these simple pleasures into your routine.

_____

_____

_____

_____

_____

_____

_____

_____

_____

_____

_____

_____

_____

_____

c. Consider the role of gratitude and joy in fostering resilience during challenging times. Write about how a positive mindset can contribute to overcoming obstacles. Develop strategies for maintaining gratitude and finding joy even in the face of difficulties.

_____

_____

_____

_____

_____

_____

_____

_____

_____

_____

_____

_____

_____

_____

_____

Chapter 9: The New Norm: Maintaining Momentum and Avoiding Relapse

Overview:

In this crucial chapter, the author guides couples in establishing a new norm for their marriage, emphasizing the importance of maintaining positive momentum and avoiding relapse into old patterns. The focus is on identifying triggers and potential setbacks, building sustainable communication and conflict resolution skills, and continuously nurturing the relationship through intentional investments. The chapter serves as a roadmap for couples to sustain the positive changes achieved in their journey of renewal.

Key Takeaways:
Identifying Triggers and Potential Setbacks
Teaching Points:
Self-Awareness and Reflection:

The chapter highlights the significance of self-awareness and reflection in identifying triggers. Couples are encouraged to explore individual and shared triggers that may lead to relapse into old behaviors or patterns.

Open Communication About Potential Setbacks:

Practical insights are provided on fostering open communication about potential setbacks. The lesson emphasizes the importance of creating a safe space for discussing triggers and collaboratively developing strategies to navigate challenges.

Main Lesson:

The author aims to convey that proactive identification of triggers is key to preventing relapse. The chapter teaches that by fostering open communication and self-awareness, couples can build resilience against potential setbacks.

a. Reflect on past challenges or relapses in your relationship. Write about the specific triggers that led to setbacks. Develop a list of potential triggers that you need to be aware of in the future.

_____

_____

_____

_____

_____

_____

_____

_____

_____

_____

_____

_____

_____

_____

b. Identify patterns of behavior or situations that have historically resulted in setbacks. Write about the impact of these patterns on your relationship. Develop strategies for recognizing and addressing these patterns proactively.

_____

_____

_____

_____

_____

_____

_____

_____

_____

_____

_____

_____

_____

_____

_____

c. Consider external factors that may contribute to relapses. Write about how changes in circumstances or stressors can affect your relationship. Develop a plan for navigating external challenges without compromising the progress you've made.

_____

_____

_____

_____

_____

_____

_____

_____

_____

_____

_____

_____

_____

_____

Building Sustainable Communication and Conflict Resolution Skills

Teaching Points:

Effective Communication Strategies:

The chapter delves into effective communication strategies that promote understanding and connection. Couples are guided to practice active listening, expressing needs and concerns constructively, and fostering a culture of openness.

Conflict Resolution Techniques:

Practical exercises are introduced to help couples build sustainable conflict resolution skills. This involves learning to navigate disagreements respectfully, finding common ground, and seeking solutions collaboratively.

Main Lesson:

Building sustainable communication and conflict resolution skills is essential for maintaining positive momentum. The chapter teaches that by cultivating effective communication habits, couples can address challenges constructively and prevent the recurrence of damaging patterns.

a. Reflect on the communication and conflict resolution skills you currently possess. Write about their effectiveness and areas for improvement. Develop specific goals for enhancing these skills to maintain healthy dynamics.

_____

_____

_____

_____

_____

_____

_____

_____

_____

_____

_____

_____

_____

_____

b. Identify recurring communication challenges in your relationship. Write about the impact of these challenges on your connection. Develop actionable steps for improving communication and conflict resolution in these specific areas.

_____

_____

_____

_____

_____

_____

_____

_____

_____

_____

_____

_____

_____

_____

c. Consider the role of active listening in sustaining momentum. Write about how truly understanding your partner contributes to a supportive environment. Develop habits for practicing active listening regularly.

_____

_____

_____

_____

_____

_____

_____

_____

_____

_____

_____

_____

_____

Continuous Nurturing and Intentional Investments in the Relationship
Teaching Points:
Consistent Relationship Nurturing:

The lesson explores the concept of continuous nurturing in the relationship. Couples are guided to make intentional investments of time, effort, and affection to foster a sense of closeness and connection.
Planning and Setting Relationship Goals:

Practical strategies are provided for setting relationship goals and plans for intentional investments. The chapter emphasizes that by actively working towards shared goals, couples can reinforce their commitment to a thriving marriage.
Main Lesson:
Continuous nurturing and intentional investments are the pillars of a sustainable relationship. The chapter teaches that by consistently prioritizing the relationship, couples can create a new norm characterized by love, understanding, and shared growth.

a. Reflect on the intentional investments you've made in your relationship so far. Write about the positive outcomes and the impact on your connection. Develop a plan for consistently nurturing the relationship through intentional actions.

_____

_____

_____

_____

_____

_____

_____

_____

_____

_____

_____

_____

_____

_____

b. Identify areas where you can deepen your emotional connection. Write about specific ways to strengthen the emotional bond with your partner. Develop rituals or practices that promote continuous nurturing.

_____

_____

_____

_____

_____

_____

_____

_____

_____

_____

_____

_____

_____

_____

c. Consider the balance between individual and shared goals. Write about how supporting each other's aspirations contributes to the overall health of the relationship. Develop strategies for aligning individual and shared investments in the future.

_____

_____

_____

_____

_____

_____

_____

_____

_____

_____

_____

_____

_____

_____

Made in the USA
Middletown, DE
24 October 2024